Next Stop:
Canada

Ginger McDonnell

Consultant

Timothy Rasinski, Ph.D.
Kent State University

Publishing Credits

Dona Herweck Rice, *Editor-in-Chief*
Robin Erickson, *Production Director*
Lee Aucoin, *Creative Director*
Conni Medina, M.A.Ed., *Editorial Director*
Jamey Acosta, *Editor*
Stephanie Reid, *Photo Editor*
Rachelle Cracchiolo, M.S.Ed., *Publisher*

Based on writing from *TIME For Kids.*

TIME For Kids and the *TIME For Kids* logo are registered trademarks of TIME Inc. Used under license.

Teacher Created Materials

5301 Oceanus Drive
Huntington Beach, CA 92649-1030
http://www.tcmpub.com

ISBN 978-1-4333-3611-9

© 2012 by Teacher Created Materials, Inc.

Table of Contents

Welcome to Canada!

Welcome to **Canada**, the North American country nearest to the North Pole!

Today Canada is its own country. Long ago, it belonged to England. Before that, it belonged to France.

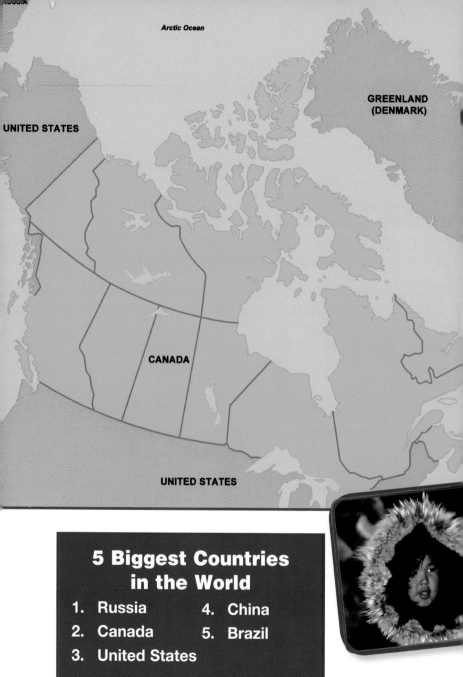

Arctic Ocean

UNITED STATES

GREENLAND
(DENMARK)

CANADA

UNITED STATES

5 Biggest Countries
in the World

1. Russia   4. China
2. Canada   5. Brazil
3. United States

Canada is the second-biggest country in the world by size. It covers most of the top of **North America**.

American Indians were the first people living in Canada. Canada's name comes from an American Indian word for *village*.

Some of the world's prettiest land is in Canada.

The north of Canada is very cold. It is often covered with snow and ice. Few people live there.

Canada has deep, green
forests. It also has tall, rocky
mountains. Mount Logan is the
tallest mountain in Canada.

There are many islands
in Canada. Sandy **shores**,
green **meadows**, and colorful
wildflowers can be found there.

Farms stretch under big,
blue skies across Canada's wide
plains.

Plants

The plains have few trees but a lot of tall **prairie** grass. There are almost no plants in the north.

In the west, thick forests are filled with evergreens like pine, spruce, and fir.

Have you ever smelled an **evergreen** forest? It has a rich, spicy smell.

Animals

Different animals live in each kind of land.

In the forests you will find
wolves, rabbits, and beavers. Deer,
foxes, and bears live there, too.

The chilly north is home to furry polar bears and **caribou**.

Narwhals live in the cold ocean there.

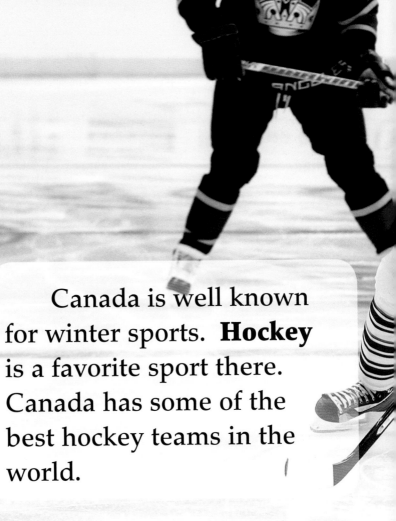

Canada is well known for winter sports. **Hockey** is a favorite sport there. Canada has some of the best hockey teams in the world.

Canadian athletes win many medals in the **Winter Olympics**. They are especially good skiers and ice skaters.

There are many big cities in Canada. Toronto is the biggest city. Ottawa is Canada's capital.

Montreal is an old city. Most people there speak French, just like the people who settled there long ago.

What else would you like to know about Canada? This chart will tell you more important facts.

Facts About Canada	
Official Language:	English and French
Leader:	prime minister
Year of Independence:	1931
Number of Provinces:	10
Number of Territories:	3
Flag:	3 stripes (red, white, red); red maple leaf in the center
Symbol:	maple leaf
Anthem:	"O, Canada"
Major Crops:	wheat, barley, corn, potatoes, soybeans
Money:	Canadian dollar

Glossary

American Indians—people whose ancestors were the first to live in the Americas

Canada—a large country in North America

caribou—a type of deer that lives in the Arctic

evergreen—a kind of plant that is green all year round

forests—areas of land with large, thick growths of trees

hockey—a sport played on ice with sticks and a puck

meadows—areas of land covered with grass

narwhals—a type of whale that lives in arctic oceans

North America—one of the seven continents of the world

plains—treeless open areas of land

prairie—a wide area of rolling grassland

shores—land along the edges of bodies of water

Winter Olympics—sport competitions played every four years by athletes from around the world